GREATEST SPORTS HEROES

Soccer Stars

Therese Shea

Children's Press®
A Division of Scholastic Inc.
New York / Toronto / London / Auckland / Sydney
Mexico City / New Delhi / Hong Kong
Danbury, Connecticut

Book Design: Dean Galiano
Contributing Editor: Karl Bollers

Photo credits: Cover © Stuart Franklin/Getty Images; p. 4 © John Moore/Getty Images; p. 7 © Brian Bahr/Getty Images; p. 8 © Mike Hewitt/Getty Images; p. 11 Richard Heathcote/Getty Images; p. 13 © John McConnico via Getty Images; p. 14 © Stand Honda/AFP/Getty Images; p. 17 © Ville Myllynen/AFP/Getty Images; p. 19 © Jim McIssac/Getty Images; p. 20 © Donald Miralle/Getty Images; p. 25 © Jed Jacobsohn/Getty Images; p. 26 © Antonio Scorza/AFP/Getty Images; p. 29 © Jean-Philippe Ksiazek/AFP/Getty Images; p. 31 © Cesar Rangel/AFP/Getty Images; p. 32 © Carl de Souza/AFP/Getty Images; p. 36 © Harry How/Getty Images; p. 40 © Filippo Monteforte/AFT/Getty Images

Library of Congress Cataloging-in-Publication Data

Shea, Therese.
 Soccer stars / Therese Shea.
 p. cm. - (Greatest sports heroes)
 Includes index.
  ISBN-10: 0-531-12588-2 (lib. bdg.)   0-531-18705-5 (pbk.)
  ISBN-13: 978-0-531-12588-5 (lib. bdg.)   978-0-531-18705-0 (pbk.)
 1. Soccer players-Biography-Juvenile literature. I. Title. II. Series.

 GV942.7.A1S48 200
 796.334092'2-dc22

                                                        2006006794

Contents

Introduction

The score is tied. There are only 30 seconds left on the clock. Suddenly, your teammate steals the ball from your opponent.

"Pass the ball to me!" you shout.

He kicks the ball to you. You start running. Two players from the opposing team race after you. You aim the ball for the net and give it your best kick. The goalie reaches out to block your shot, but misses it by an inch! You scored a goal!

Professional soccer stars often experience exciting moments like this. Playing soccer is fun, but it's hard work, too. Soccer players must be able to run the length of the soccer field. They must master difficult skills, such as kicking, dribbling, and heading. Dribbling is moving a ball by tapping, bouncing, or kicking. Heading is driving a soccer ball by hitting it with the head.

Soccer is such a popular sport that it is played in countries all over the world.

A soccer team has eleven players. Each team has one goalkeeper and anywhere from one to three forwards, three to six midfielders, and three to five defenders.

Forwards, or attackers, are the offense, players whose main job is to score. They need to be fast enough to get past their opponents. They also need to be able to kick the ball past the goalkeeper. Midfielders are most often in the middle of the field. They play offense and defense. Midfielders are skilled at passing and scoring.

Defensive players keep opponents from scoring. The goalkeeper stands in front of the net and tries to stop a ball from going into the goal. Defenders, sometimes called fullbacks or defensive backs, try to take the ball before the opponent scores.

Soccer, or football as it is called outside of the United States, is possibly the most popular sport on the planet. Let's meet some of the world's greatest soccer stars and learn why soccer is one of today's most exciting sports!

It takes lots of practice and determination to develop the skills needed to be a soccer star.

Chapter One

David Beckham

"As soon as I hit the ball, I know if it's in."
—*David Beckham*

Even people who are not soccer fans know David Beckham. David grew up playing soccer for fun. He was born in London, England, on May 2, 1975. His parents were huge soccer fans. The whole family would travel great distances to see their favorite professional soccer club, Manchester United.

David started playing on his local youth team when he was seven years old. In three years, he scored 100 goals! On his fourteenth birthday, David signed a contract with Manchester United in England's Premier League. At first, he played with their youth club. In 1992, the team won the Football Association (FA) Youth Cup, a national title, for the first time since 1964!

Soccer star David Beckham has been playing the sport ever since he was a kid!

In 1993, David was invited into Manchester United's professional club as a midfielder. He played his first game in the 1994–1995 season. In that game against Turkey, he scored United's only goal. This was the first of many goals in David's brilliant career. David helped Manchester United win the Premier League championship the next year.

On The Ball

The earliest mention of a soccerlike game dates back over four thousand years to ancient China. The ancient Greeks, Romans, and Vikings also played ball-kicking games.

Soccer-crazy fans pack stadiums and follow the action on television in amazing numbers. The record for the biggest crowd at a soccer game is 199,854! This game was between Brazil and Uruguay, played in the Maracanã Municipal Stadium in Rio de Janeiro, Brazil, in 1950. The 2002 World Cup was broadcast on television in 213 countries around the world and seen by over twenty-eight billion people!

David Beckham's fans can hardly contain their excitement, as he gets ready to "bend" the ball.

David is known for "bending" the ball. He kicks the ball so that it curves through the air as it soars toward the goal. Goalkeepers can't predict where it will land.

David has won many awards, including the 1997 Union of European Football Association's (UEFA) Best Midfielder, the 1999 UEFA Most Valuable Player, and the Sports Writers' Association's 2001 Sportsman of the Year.

In 2000, Beckham was named captain of England's national soccer team. He helped them qualify for the 2002 World Cup with a free kick in a match against Greece. A free kick is a kick that is given to a team if the team's opponent commits an illegal action.

David played with Manchester United for thirteen years. During that time, they won six Premier League championships, two Football Association (FA) Cups, and one UEFA Champions League title.

In 2003, David Beckham signed a four-year contract with a team called Real Madrid of Spain. He proved to be a key player for them. They won the UEFA Super Cup that year.

David is married with three children. David likes to help others. One of his proudest moments was being asked to be a United Nations Children's Fund (UNICEF) Goodwill Ambassador in 2005.

Goal Nugget

Beckham chose the number 23 for his Real Madrid jersey. He liked this number because it was worn by basketball star Michael Jordan.

As a UNICEF Goodwill Ambassador, David works to improve the lives of children all over the world.

Chapter Two

Freddy Adu

"I love having the ball at my feet . . . that's when I'm at my best, when I can pull some weird move . . . and everyone goes, 'Ohhhhhh.' I love that."

—Freddy Adu

Freddy Adu amazes everyone with his soccer talents. In 2004, he became the youngest person in the United States to play professional soccer. He was only fourteen!

Freddy was born June 2, 1989, in Ghana in western Africa. By age six, he was playing soccer in his neighborhood. Freddy's mother, Emelia, won a visa in the U.S. Green Card Lottery when he was eight. A visa is a document that allows a person to enter and remain in a country for a certain amount of time. This meant Freddy's family could move to the United States.

As a boy living in Ghana, Freddy Adu often played soccer in his bare feet

Freddy's family settled in Maryland. In fourth grade, Freddy met the coach of the Potomac Tigers, who signed Freddy immediately.

In 2002, Freddy moved to Florida to attend a school run by the U.S. Soccer Federation. He soon became a member of the U.S. Under-17 National Team. This team has the best under-seventeen players in the nation.

The next year, his team qualified for the Under-17 World Cup in Finland. In his first World Cup game, Freddy scored 3 goals. He was then asked to join the U.S. Under-20 National Team in the World Youth Championship. Freddy was named U.S. Soccer Young Male Athlete of 2003.

Many people were watching Freddy's performances. He received an offer to play

Goal Nugget

The World Cup is an international soccer tournament. It takes place every four years. Over two hundred teams compete for the championship. The competitions begin about two years before the final game!

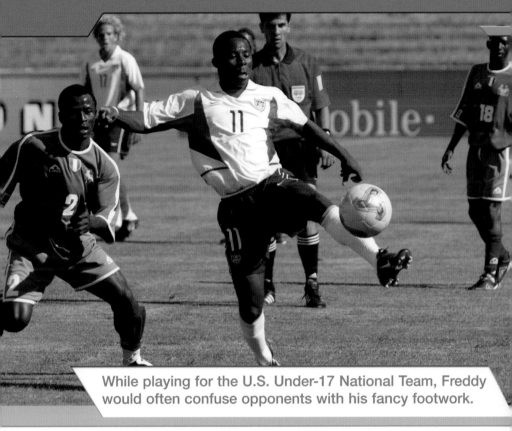

While playing for the U.S. Under-17 National Team, Freddy would often confuse opponents with his fancy footwork.

Major League Soccer (MLS) for the Washington, D.C.-based D.C. United in November 2003.

D.C. United selected Freddy as the first pick in the player draft that year. A draft is a system in which players are picked by professional sports teams. Just fourteen, he was the youngest player ever to play in this league. He was also the highest paid, earning over $500,000 a year!

Freddie continued to play for the U.S. under-20 national team in 2004, as well as for D.C. United. He played so well he was the Commissioner's Pick in the MLS All-Star game.

Freddy is known for his fast feet. He can easily "fake" a move. This means he pretends he is moving the ball one way but really moves it the other way. The defender is put off balance and confused.

Freddy still acts like a normal kid. He likes golf and playing video games. He is happy to be playing the sport he loves.

Many people have a difficult time believing that Freddy could be so young and talented.

"I'm going to keep playing until I can't contribute anymore."

— Kristine Lilly

Someday you may drive into the town of Wilton, Connecticut. If you do, you will see a sign that reads, "Hometown of Olympic gold medalist Kristine Lilly." Gold medals are only the beginnings of Kristine's accomplishments.

Kristine was born July 22, 1971, in New York City. By age six, Kristine was already a determined soccer player. There were no girls' soccer teams where her family lived, so she played on the local boys' team!

The Lilly family moved to Wilton several years later. Kristine made the high school varsity team when she was just a freshman. Her team won three state championships during her four years of school. Kristine was invited onto the U.S. Women's Under-19

Kristine Lilly has played in more international matches than any other player in soccer history!

National Team when she was fifteen years old.

Kristine attended the University of North Carolina. Her school soccer team captured four national championships during her four years on North Carolina's offense.

Kristine was the first college player to be first-team all-American four years in a row. An all-American is a person chosen to be the best in his or her sport in the United States.

Kristine played on the U.S. Women's National Team when they won the World Cup in 1991. In fact, she has played in more international games than any other man or woman in soccer history. Kristine was the U.S. Soccer Female Athlete of the Year in 1993. Three years later, she helped the United States win the gold medal for women's soccer in the 1996 Atlanta Olympics.

Goal Nugget

Kristine Lilly's high school named its soccer field after her!

In the 1999 World Cup play-off game, Kristine was named Most Valuable Player as the United States captured another world championship. She made a well-known defensive play during this game. She blocked a header by a Chinese player that would have been the winning goal. This tournament excited many Americans about women's soccer for the first time and interested many young girls in playing the sport.

In 2004, Kristine once more helped the United States win the Olympic gold medal in women's soccer. She continues to break records on the women's national team. She is called the "Iron Woman" because she has played more minutes of professional soccer than any other player, male or female. She is also the second-leading point scorer in U.S. women's soccer history and has over 100 goals.

Kristine is not a flashy player. She quietly defends and scores. Many of her teammates consider her the backbone of the team.

Kristine likes to keep her skills sharp between national team play. She once played in a men's indoor soccer league. Finally, she helped start the Women's United Soccer Association (WUSA). She was an all-star during the three years she played with the Boston Breakers.

In 2005, Kristine was named the U.S. Soccer Female Athlete of the Year for the second time! She is the current captain of the national team. Kristine continues to encourage young girls to follow their dreams with the Kristine Lilly Soccer Camp. She is living proof that women can achieve athletic greatness, too.

Kristine brings heart and soul to every game
practice and match in which she participates.

Chapter Four

Ronaldinho

"Ronaldinho is an incredible player. He is a great footballer, and a great person."

—David Beckham

Ronaldinho (ro-nal-deen-yo) likes to say that he was born with a ball at his feet. This midfielder's natural talent makes you believe him. He seems unstoppable.

Ronaldinho's real name is Ronaldo de Assis Moreira, but he is known as Ronaldinho all over the world. This means "little Ronaldo." He was born March 21, 1980, in Porto Alegre, Brazil. His first taste of fame came when he was just thirteen years old. Ronaldinho was featured in a newspaper for scoring 23 goals in one soccer match!

Ronaldinho won a spot on Brazil's Under-17 national team in 1997. That year, Brazil won the Under-17 World Cup with Ronaldinho as the top scorer. He became a professional

Ronaldinho is a serious and dedicated professional who spends hours perfecting his technique.

player in 1998 with a Brazilian team called Gremio. He played three years for this team.

During this time, he also began to play with the senior Brazil national team. He proved to be an amazing midfielder and forward. He received much attention from European soccer clubs. Ronaldinho left his home country in 2001 to play for Paris Saint-Germain in France. He said his time in France helped him grow as a player.

On The Ball

Ronaldinho isn't the first soccer star to hail from Brazil. Many people consider Brazilian soccer champion Pelé to be the greatest player ever. He led the Santos Football Club to nine championships from 1956 to 1974. He led Brazil's national team to four World Cups, winning three. Pelé scored 1,283 goals throughout his career. From 1975 to 1977 he played for the New York Cosmos in the North American Soccer League. The National Olympic Committee named Pelé Athlete of the Century.

Ronaldinho (center) has established himself as Brazil's leading goal scorer.

Ronaldinho's best games continued to be with his Brazilian national team. In the 2002 World Cup quarterfinals against England, Ronaldinho stunned the world. He scored a goal 115 feet (35 meters) from the net! Brazil went on to win the World Cup.

In 2003, Ronaldinho left his Paris team to play for Football Club (FC) Barcelona in Spain's Primera division. He immediately helped his team with his complicated footwork and scoring ability. By the end of the 2003–2004 season, Barcelona had risen from the bottom of the standings to second place in their league. The team also won an outstanding seventeen games in a row! Ronaldinho was named the 2004 Fédération Internationale de Football Association (FIFA) World Player of the Year.

Ronaldinho showed no signs of slowing down in 2005. Barcelona won the Primera League Championship and the Spanish Super Cup. He captained the Brazilian national team to win the Confederations Cup tournament. He was also named the FIFA World Player of the Year again as well as European Footballer of the Year.

Ronaldinho says he is the happiest man in the world when he has the ball. Only in his mid-twenties, he is certain to stay the happiest man for years to come!

Ronaldinho's opponents are amazed at his incredible skills!

Chapter Five

Andriy Shevchenko

"I don't like to lose very much. I'm a fighter. I will struggle to the end."

—*Andriy Shevchenko*

"Sheva!" That's the name shouted by millions of soccer fans around the world. "Sheva" is Andriy Shevchenko's nickname. He was born September 29, 1976, in Kiev, the capital of Ukraine, in the former Soviet Union. He has become one of the most popular soccer players in the world.

Sheva played soccer at school and for a local team. A scout, or person hired to locate talented athletes, spotted him when he was nine years old. This scout wanted him to train for the city team, Dynamo Kiev. However, a major event interrupted Sheva's training.

In 1986, an accident took place at a nuclear power plant in the town of Chernobyl. A nuclear power plant is a place where energy is produced by splitting atoms of a certain element. Thousands of families, including

Andriy Shevchenko combines speed, skill, and a sharp eye for the goal.

Sheva's, had to move away from the danger zone. After a few months, though, Sheva returned to play soccer for the Dynamo junior team. In 1994, Sheva became a forward on the Dynamo senior team. Ukrainian players named him Newcomer of the Year (1995–1996).

Footballer of the Year

In 1996, Dynamo played in the UEFA Champions League tournament. Sheva became the first Ukrainian player to score a hat trick, or three goals during one game, in the Champions League. He has been named Ukrainian Footballer of the Year by newspapers and other professionals every year since 1996!

In July 1999, he signed with Athletic Club (AC) Milan in the Italian soccer league called

Goal Nugget

During the Ian Rush Tournament, young Sheva's ability to score was so impressive that Welsh soccer great Ian Rush awarded him a pair of soccer shoes.

Serie A. By the end of the season, Sheva led the league in goals with 24 goals in 32 games.

One of Sheva's most famous moments came in 2003. AC Milan had reached Italy's Champions League tournament final against Juventus. The teams were tied after overtime. During the shoot-out, Sheva kicked in the winning goal. A shoot-out occurs at the end of a tied game.

By the end of the 2003–2004 season, Sheva was again the league's top scorer. He kicked in the only goal of the UEFA Super Cup finals.

Helping Others

Sheva has won many awards. He has even been named a "Hero of Ukraine," and for good reason. Sheva began an organization called the Andriy Shevchenko Foundation. A foundation is an organization that is created to make sure money and services are given to a cause. This foundation works to improve the lives of poor children in Ukraine. Sheva will continue to play with Milan until at least 2009. He has said that he has not yet reached his best. If this is true, he will be an exciting player to watch in the future!

"Abby has the ability to beat you in so many ways. She has great size, great leaping ability, and deceptively good speed."

—Mia Hamm

When Abby Wambach has the ball, defenders are afraid to get in her way. Why? Because she will either outrun them or take them down.

Abby was born on June 2, 1980, in Pittsford, New York. She is the youngest of seven children. She was always playing sports with her older brothers and sisters. She joined her first soccer league when she was four years old. When Abby was nine, a coach suggested putting her on a boys' team.

In 1997, Abby was the National High School Player of the Year. Many colleges wanted her to play for them. Abby chose the University of Florida.

Abby Wambach has been attracting attention on the soccer field since childhood.

Abby was a success on the field in Florida. She made the all-conference team four years in a row, Conference Player of the Year twice, and took her team to the National College Athletic Association (NCAA) Final Four tournament in 2001. She set many records at the University of Florida, including most goals, assists, and hat tricks. An assist is a pass that results in a goal.

National Team All-Star

Abby began playing for the U.S. Women's National Team in 2001. In 2002, she played seven games, scored 5 goals, and had four assists. In 2003, the team qualified for the Women's World Cup. Abby scored the most goals on the U.S. team.

Abby also played with the WUSA for the Washington Freedom starting in 2002. She was the Rookie of the Year. During the two years she was with the team, she was an all-star.

The year 2004 was one of Abby's best on the national team. She fulfilled her dream and played in the 2004 Olympic Games. She became the first U.S. player to score four goals during the competition. Abby helped her team to the gold when she scored in overtime against Brazil. Abby was then named the 2004 U.S. Soccer Female Athlete of the Year for the second year in a row.

Abby is not just known in the United States. She was fourth place for the 2004 FIFA Women's World Player of the Year. She also played in the Women's World Stars game in Paris as a forward and as a midfielder.

Abby Wambach trains hard but she can relax, too. She is known for playing jokes on her teammates. They are often amazed that she can be so fun and yet so tough on the field. At home, she likes to play video games, listen to music, and read books. Like Kristine Lilly, Abby wants other girls to have the opportunity to play soccer well. She returns home to Pittsford, New York, every summer to run a soccer camp for girls.

Chapter Seven

Stars of Tomorrow

Most soccer stars are born with talent. The best ones work hard to make this talent something more. The soccer stars of today all started practicing at a very young age. The same is true of tomorrow's soccer stars.

Christian Maldini, whose father and grandfather both were professional soccer players for Italy's AC Milan, already plays on the AC Milan juvenile squad at age nine.

The Brazilian soccer team, Santos, and England's Manchester United were so greatly impressed by the skill of nine-year-old Jean Carlos Chera from Brazil that both teams competed for the right to train him. Santos eventually won.

Christian and Jean Carlos will practice hard and learn much during the coming years. The most important lesson they will learn is that soccer is a team sport. It takes eleven players to win a game.

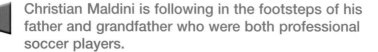

Christian Maldini is following in the footsteps of his father and grandfather who were both professional soccer players.

New Words

all-American (**awl**-uh-**mer**-ih-kuhn) a person who is chosen to be the best in his or her sport in the United States

assist (uh-**sisst**) a pass that results in a goal

commissioner (kuh-**mish**-uh-ner) the head of a professional sport

contract (**kon**-trakt) an official, written agreement between two or more people or groups

defense (di-**fens**) the members of a team attempting to keep an opponent from scoring in a game

draft (**draft**) a system by which new players are selected for professional sports teams

dribbling (**drib**-ling) to move a ball by tapping, bouncing, or kicking with a foot or feet

foundation (foun-**day**-shuhn) an organization created to make sure that money and services are given to a cause

New Words

free kick (free kik) a kick allowed to a team if the opponent commits an illegal action

hat trick (hat trik) the act of scoring three goals in one game by one player

heading (hed-ing) to drive a soccer ball by hitting it with one's head

offense (aw-fenss) the members of a team attempting to score

qualify (kwahl-uh-fye) to perform well enough to compete in a contest

scout (skout) a person hired to locate talented athletes

shoot-out (shoot-out) an event that occurs when a game is tied and time has run out; each team receives a number of chances to score

visa (vee-zuh) a document that allows the bearer to enter and remain in a country for an amount of time

For Further Reading

Gifford, Clive. Soccer: *The Ultimate Guide to the Beautiful Game.* Boston: Houghton Mifflin, 2004.

Hornby, Hugh. *Soccer.* New York: Dorling Kindersley, 2000.

Roza, Greg. *David Beckham: Soccer Superstar.* New York: The Rosen Publishing Group, Inc., 2006.

Rutledge, Rachel. *The Best of the Best in Soccer.* Brookfield, CT: The Millbrook Press, 1998.

Sullivan, George. *All About Soccer.* New York: G.P. Putnam's Sons, 2001.

Resources

ORGANIZATIONS

Fédération Internationale de Football Association (FIFA)
Hitzigweg 11, P.O. Box 85,
8030 Zurich, Switzerland
Phone: (41) 43/222-7777
http://www.fifa.com

Major League Soccer
420 Fifth Avenue
New York, NY 10018
E-mail: feedback@mlsnet.com
http://www.mlsnet.com

U.S. Soccer Federation
1801 S. Prairie Ave.
Chicago, IL 60616
Phone: (312) 808-1300
http://www.ussoccer.com

Resources

Scholastic: The World of Soccer
http://teacher.scholastic.com/scholasticnews/
indepth/soccer2005/soccerstories/
This informative Web site details the history of
soccer, the rules of the sport, soccer news,
and current events.

The Online David Beckham Fanzine
http://www.beckham-magazine.com

The Official Kristine Lilly Website
http://www.kristinelilly13.com/

Abby Wambach: The Official Website
http://www.abbywambach.com/

Samba Foot: Ronaldinho
http://ronaldinho.sambafoot.com/en/

Index

Index

ABOUT THE AUTHOR

Therese Shea lives and writes in Buffalo, New York. A graduate of Providence College and the State University of New York at Buffalo, she is the author of several books.